No-nonsense project audi
for the

By

Lisa Nash

No-nonsense project auditing: A practical guide for the PMO
Author: Lisa Nash

The advice and strategies contained herein may not be suitable for every situation. Neither the publisher nor the author shall be liable for damages arising here from. The fact that an organisation or website is referred to in this work as a citation and/or a potential source of further information does not mean that the author or the publisher endorses the information, the organisation or website may provide or recommendations it may make.

The author and publisher reserve the right to make any changes they deem necessary to future versions of the publication to ensure its accuracy. The reader assumes all responsibility for the use of the information within this book. While every precaution has been taken in the preparation of this book, the publisher and author assume no responsibility for errors or omissions, or for injuries, losses, untoward results, or any other damages that may result from the use of information in this book.

The moral right of the author has been asserted.

Published by: LMN Associates LTD
Cover Design by: Brianna Perez

www.pmosynergy.com
Follow the author @PMOSynergy

ISBN E-book: 9780993403538
ISBN Paperback: 9780993403521

Contents

· ·

Introduction

. . . .

I am a Project, Programme and Portfolio Management office (PMO) Consultant with over 15 years professional experience. I have worked in a variety of organisations in different industries and sectors during this time with different levels of maturity, some with established PMO's and some with nothing in place at all.

I have written this book as a means to help other people in the industry. I was finding myself being asked questions and advice and for a long time have wanted to put the results of my experience down onto paper to share what I know.

This book is part two of a four part series. Book one ("Level up your PMO: 6 tips to make your PMO a success" which can be found on the amazon store) was designed primarily for permanent or interim Senior PMO analysts looking to make the move to PMO Manager as well as permanent or interim PMO Managers that were new to the role although it could also benefit those same managers looking to improve what they already do. Whilst it was a guide, everyone has different ways of doing things, and this book approaches auditing in the same way.

About this book

This book is designed to be an informal, simple, real-world approach and reference guide to auditing quality in projects. It is primarily designed for:

- Permanent or interim PMO Managers leading an audit

- Permanent or interim PMO analysts (at all levels) taking part in audits
- Anyone else that wants to know more about how project audits can be approached

It is for those that want some industry insight and guidance in this field. It is not aligned to any specific quality standard and is not intended to replace or compete with any of the existing standards such as BSI (British Standards Institute) and ISO (International Organisation for Standardisation). This no-nonsense approach has been designed to obtain a level of information in order to make decisions. This includes:

- Understanding what projects are about, where they are in their lifecycle and their general state of health.
- Identifying what the biggest project issues are, as well as areas to target for recovery and improvement.
- Discovering the level of adherence and compliance to project process and methodology

Terms and Explanations

The book primarily refers to projects, and the reader should take this to mean one project, a project as part of a programme or a project as part of a portfolio. Where it talks about more than one project, there are specific references included.

In addition, the word 'PMO' may sometimes be used instead of 'PMO Team' or 'PMO Manager' but the context of the sentence will be clear about which one is being referred to.

Be sure to check the glossary at the back for additional explanations of certain terms if required. The search function on e-readers can also be used to find certain words or phrases throughout the book.

Methodologies

Understanding the methodology is vital in order to know the approach, processes, standards and therefore the documentation that will be audited. Throughout the book, it mainly refers to and is aimed at users of waterfall or hybrid waterfall-agile project methodologies although there is some reference to pure agile methods as well.

Navigating around this book

Certain icons and ways of presenting information have been used in this book to help the reader to distinguish and find certain kinds of information that may be of use. These include:

 The bulb icon indicates a helpful tip or idea

 The exclamation mark indicates a friendly warning or something to take note of

 The world icon indicates an internet web reference that might be useful.

Please note that diagrams in this book may be harder to see on an e-reader, and so copies have been provided at my website for free (links included throughout the book). There is also a link available for free for all readers at the end to an audit ready template which contains the guide criteria within this book.

Questions, comments, feedback, advice

If you have any questions, comments, or feedback about this book, or would like some support, guidance or advice on implementing or improving the PMO within your organisation, please get in touch via www.pmosynergy.com.

Chapter 1

Auditing and the five w's –
who, what, when, where, why

Why do it?

The word 'PMO' stands for 'Project, Programme, or Portfolio Management Office' and performs different functions depending on the level it is positioned at based on management and organisational need.

According to UK based company Axelos' global best practice standard 'P3O', PMO's provide 'a decision enabling/delivery support structure for all change within an organisation…(and) create(s) tailored governance and support structures for managing portfolios, programmes and projects'[1].

---

[1] Axelos advise that P3O builds on the references in PRINCE2®, Managing Successful Programmes (MSP®), Management of Risk (M_o_R®) and Management of Portfolios (MoP®) to provide a single information source for organisations or individuals wishing to set up or maintain an effective delivery support office. The Axelos website with these details and links to manuals and training can be found at https://www.axelos.com/best-practice-solutions/p3o.

Using this definition then, audit results can help the PMO to improve and streamline governance and support structures, improve project and programme management maturity and growth, facilitate better decision making and provide targeted and value-add delivery support.

Project auditing should be a standard and regular activity in every PMO regardless of its level, whether that be project, programme, portfolio or enterprise. It is a useful tool to develop a familiarity about and determine the health of a project or set of projects, to discover compliance and adherence to project process as well as to enable the ability to look for ways to improve project, programme or portfolio health and processes and determine a plan for recovery if appropriate.

Understanding project health helps to build knowledge around whether projects are on track to achieve their targets and objectives. If during an audit it is discovered that projects are not on track or are looking particularly risky, the PMO can then use this information to assist in taking action to either bring it back on track, reduce the risk, or to stop it altogether (with stakeholder decision making) if it is no longer viable. Over time, this data can be used to facilitate continuous improvement within departments, teams, and organisations.

Documents, or anything that provides information or communication about something on a project, gives the PMO the necessary evidence of activity and knowledge about progress. In an agile environment, some evidence may not materialise in the form of what people traditionally see as a 'document', but the PMO may use agile software tools (such as Jira or Rally) to obtain information, view the information boards (usually populated with post-it notes) produced by agile teams, talk to Project Managers or Scrum Masters or even attend as an observer at a daily stand up as a way to understand what is going on.

Audits bring information, and with information comes the ability to make decisions or take necessary actions if appropriate. Since one of the responsibilities of the PMO is to ensure projects are controlled, governed and monitored correctly, auditing becomes an essential for the PMO's toolkit.

Who should conduct it?

It is recommended that the audit be lead by someone who has at least five to ten years PMO experience, because this person should be the one to define, set and improve audit criteria and be able to coach and lead the team to follow the standards required. It is also helpful if that person also has experience of managing projects, as this enables the person to have a fully rounded view, be fully aware of what to expect, be very clear about what they are looking for but also know what it is like to be on both auditor and auditee sides.

If there is more than one person in the PMO, the audit should be conducted as a group, as this enables consistency in approach at other review times (such as in gate reviews which can be seen as just mini audits), but it can also be useful to bounce ideas off each other to obtain different points of view, advice and opinion, particularly if there is any confusion over a particular area. Furthermore, it helps the team to grow in terms of their collective knowledge of open projects within their remit as well as knowledge about project management and PMO process.

When should an audit be scheduled?

Whether it is the first time that an audit has been conducted (either because the PMO Manager is new, the function or team is new, or PMO audit requirements have changed), or not, some time should be given between the notice that an audit is going to take place and actually delving into documentation. This is to ensure that anyone responsible for providing information be given a chance to either produce or update documentation, or discuss what is required of them.

It is recommended that a communication goes out to auditees at least two to four weeks before the audit commences, and again a week before to remind people if this is the first time an audit is being held. However, if there is a good level of project management maturity (which can be assessed through the P3M3 model), it is not necessary to leave this much time as people will already be largely prepared; one to two weeks is best in this instance.

<u>Where</u> should an audit be held?

Audits need concentration and privacy, as there may be topics of conversation that are not suited to an open office. Depending on the amount of projects (and how new team members are to the organisation or PMO), it might also take a while to get through everything, so a separate, quiet but airy room near to the main working area are the best conditions in which to conduct an audit. If there are enough projects to justify it and as long as there is network access, I usually hold mine off site if I can to get the team away from the hustle and bustle of the office which gives a focus and importance to the day.

Less experienced members of the team should sit in close proximity to those with more experience to facilitate a collaborative working environment where people can learn from each other.

What should accompany an audit?

When about to undertake an audit, some quality criteria around success factors (what is required in order for an audit to be considered successful) needs to be summarised and understood by the people taking part and the people subject to the audit. The following is required:

- Advanced warning of an audit to Project and Programme Managers
- Why exactly the audit is taking place, what its purpose is and what the outputs are
- Who will be subject to an audit and who won't be
- What criteria will be used to assess any documentational evidence
- What documents will be assessed and judged against that criteria
- Who will receive the results of that audit and what will be done with that information
- Managers of Project and Programme manager approval or buy-in (where appropriate)

Be aware that an audit can be seen as disruptive. People should be doing what needs to be done already, but some may not, and assumptions about why that is will need to be validated before any action is taken. It might need additional time to bring documentation and other evidence up to a standard, particularly if the PMO is new or operating new processes and schedules for audits, and people may need help on understanding what they need to do to be 'audit ready'. It is therefore prudent to make sure that any managers of Project and Programme Managers agree with and buy into the audit schedule set by the PMO and understand what is being asked of their teams.

This needs to be done because any resulting issues around compliance or capability may need to be addressed by them if necessary or appropriate. It is also crucial for the PMO to approach audits in the most supportive way possible, with an open door to help Project and Programme managers where required.

<u>How</u> should results be presented?

When understanding the results of an audit, there should be an emphasis on areas that are doing well and areas that 'require improvement' rather than pointing out failure; essentially it is about 'fact finding' and not 'fault finding'. It is vital to ensure that as well as understanding what is going wrong, that success is also celebrated and people are recognised for compliance and capability; this often enables opportunities to be created for those individuals who consistently perform well.

By highlighting 'improvement areas' (meaning improvement that is needed against set criteria or standards, assuming these are in place), it puts results in kinder terms and allows people to see the gap between what they have done and what more might be required from them. Talking about failure and 'doing things wrong' can be insulting to people who are trying hard to do what is required and to do a good job, and won't build good relationships between the PMO and the project community.

The key to the presentation of results lies in how the PMO deals with specific people before telling senior and/or line management about performance. Any improvement discussion after an audit face to face and one on one can firstly ensure that relationships develop in a positive way but can also assure management that the PMO is capable of handling issues of compliance themselves.

Once these discussions have been had, the PMO may want to physically present the results on paper to management, but any negative feedback can be caveated with comments that the PMO is working with specific individuals and improvement measures have been implemented.

Escalation to line managers, where appropriate, should only be made when multiple (and creatively different) attempts to work with individuals have yielded no tangible improvement.

Please also see Chapter four, 'Creating the post audit report' for more information in this area.

Why prioritisation and sizing of projects helps with auditing

Prioritisation and assessment of projects is normally a key feature of portfolio management (but is also used for programmes), and is completed after the project business case has been approved and before the project starts. It is simply the act of deciding what comes before or after something else using pre-defined criteria to understand (but is not limited to) a projects level of risk, its financial value, the benefits it will deliver, its level of complexity, and its strategic importance which can also be used to determine a projects overall 'size', i.e. whether it is small, medium or large.

When a mechanism is put in place to decide what projects are worth doing over others and what brings the greatest benefit and therefore success to an organisation, this can ensure not only that resource is diverted to projects considered to be 'important' rather than ones that won't actually provide much of a long term return for the organisation, but can also help to determine the path and focus on projects, and whether they need a light touch governance approach (because they are small and not as risky so don't need as much deliberation or rigour) or a full governance approach (because they are risky and strategically important to the organisation and therefore require greater scrutiny and assurance).

This is particularly important with a programme or portfolio of more than one project, where competition may exist over resources including funds, people, systems and infrastructure. This also includes the resources available to provide independent oversight and assurance in a PMO.

The act of prioritisation, assessment and sizing is completed before the project starts to deliver in order to determine where it sits in the priority 'list'. With the help of assessment alongside key stakeholders (such as sponsors or business directors), a comparison can then be made between projects as to how important they are and can then be prioritised, assessed and sized.

If a project has been assessed and deemed of high importance, and during delivery this changes (because, for example, the benefits will no longer be delivered as expected or has grown to become unacceptably risky), this in itself is a reason to pause for reflection or stop the project altogether. The PMO can spot those changes (if they have not already been identified) during reviews and audits and can provide the necessary information to the relevant stakeholders who can make decisions about whether they want the project to carry on or not.

Furthermore, the PMO can spend more time and resource focussing on higher priority projects because doing so is more important to the stakeholders that prioritised them in the first place.

Making the distinction of size is crucial. Concentrating on smaller, less risky pieces of change rather than on larger, more strategically important projects is in itself a reason that people then fail to see PMO value. When important projects start to fail or lose control, if attention has been diverted to the wrong places, the PMO does have a part to play in that.

Since the practice of prioritisation and assessment is a feature of portfolio management, it usually requires a portfolio management, business relationship or business partnering function to engage Senior and Executive level stakeholders and sponsors. Their job is to liaise with those people and understand what prioritisation means for them using criteria to assess where the greatest benefits and value in the portfolio can be derived.

It is advisable for the PMO to be part of or symbiotic with such functions in order to integrate the pipeline approval processes into the project lifecycle. In the absence of these functions, the PMO may perform this role partially or fully themselves, depending on the needs of the organisation.

To summarise, prioritisation, assessment and sizing can help to determine:

- What to focus on and what not to focus so much on in audits.

- Whether, at review and audit points, projects have ongoing justification, viability and whether its priority should remain the same throughout its lifecycle.

- Whether to employ a light touch or full governance approach and understanding how much resource to apply to governance when reviewing and auditing projects.

What is the PMO fundamentally looking for?

There are three key things the PMO should keep in mind when thinking about the reasons for conducting an audit.

The first thing is to look for the presence of evidence (which may come in the form of documentation or some other medium) that indicates activity, communication and progress during the project lifecycle.

In order to know whether evidence is present or not, the PMO needs to make clear where to store it, what needs to be put there, to what level of quality and the timing for delivery. The PMO also needs to make sure that people know that they are there to help if there are any questions or confusion over those areas.

In some organisations, they link this sort of requirement for compliance to personal objectives and in others they rely on management commitment and buy-in to cascade down in a 'lead by example' type method. Both of those require a certain amount of maturity in an organisation but it is not impossible for the PMO to work towards those goals using positive relationship building.

The second thing is to understand what is going on in a project through that evidence, and being the 'independent assurance' to both the project community and relevant stakeholders, identifying any further opportunities or risk, helping to support delivery where required and providing information that enables decision making.

The third, is to understand and interpret the quality of evidence and documentation produced which can help to identify:

- Compliance or adherence to methodology or issues with it

- Project Management capability or issues with it

- Maturity growth or setbacks within project or programme management.

Knowing all of this can enable actions to be taken to improve those areas.

In Summary:

There are important elements to consider when preparing for an audit, including:

- Why you are doing it
- Who should conduct it
- When it should be scheduled
- Where it should be held
- What needs to be in place in order that it can happen
- How results should be presented
- Whether projects have been prioritised and risk assessed in order to understand the full deep dive or light touch approach to governance and auditing
- What the PMO is really looking for

Compliance and capability cannot be expected though, if the required project standards, guidelines and criteria are not in place. Furthermore, looking into why people may not be complying and being sensitive to that is also important. Reasons can include:

- People being under inordinate amounts of pressure for whatever reason.
- Dispensation may have been given under special circumstances not to produce certain project documentation.
- Low management commitment to what the PMO is there to do; compliance is also likely to be lower in this instance.

- Other things the PMO might not yet be aware of but can be discovered through talking to people or listening to what others are saying.

The PMO needs to make sure that they have the relevant buy in from the relevant stakeholders, that everyone is clear about what is expected of them before being subject to an audit, and that the PMO tries to understand reasons behind what is happening rather than labelling failure.

Chapter 2

Defining quality criteria

....

The crucial point about auditing is having quality criteria with which to measure against so that a judgement can be made about progress, fitness for purpose, and adherence to standards.

As an everyday example, there is unwritten 'MoSCoW prioritised' universal quality criteria which everyone expects in order for a table to be functional and to act as 'a table'.

MoSCoW is a prioritisation technique used to determine the importance of something and employing it ensures that stakeholders hold the same perception with regards to the view around that importance. The letters in MoSCoW stand for:

- (M)ust have
- (S)hould have
- (C)ould have
- (W)ill not have

The following criteria demonstrates that in order to be fit for purpose, a table universally must possess the following 'must-haves':

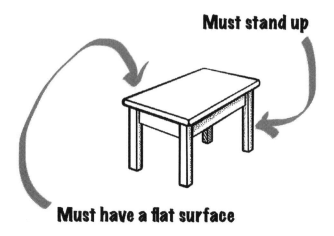

Must stand up

Must have a flat surface

In auditing, MoSCoW prioritising what requirements are in project process, methodology use and the expectations around documentation and provision of evidence of project activity can mean that people are clear about what is absolutely expected and where flexibility in these areas lay.

When judging whether the table is a table, the two points stated in the table diagram must be present in order for that to be the case. The 'standard' in this context is the universal one that everyone is familiar with and expects. If the table does not stand up independently or you cannot put things on it, the table is not generically considered fit for purpose, and then action can be taken to fix it, or do something else with it (e.g. get rid of it or use the material for another purpose).

The point being made here is that judgement can not be made as to whether something is good or bad, right or wrong, positive or negative, until there is criteria (usually aligned to a particular standard if one exists) in place which enables a differentiation to be made. The diagram below demonstrates this:

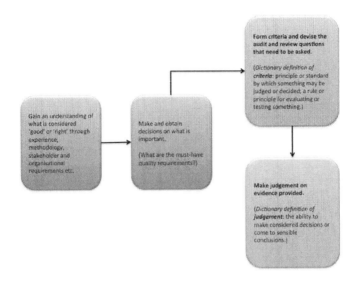

The diagram above demonstrates what conditions need to be met before criteria can be formed and judgement can then be made.

The benefit of experience allows quick judgement to be made about quality without writing down criteria, but the perception of quality between one person and another can vary considerably. This is due to the fact that people have different backgrounds, different upbringings, and different levels of experience. For example, walking into a room and knowing it is dark or light, is because people 'know' what those two things are and can immediately make a judgement without having to refer to any standard; however, that would still have had to have been learned at some point.

Writing down and MoSCoW prioritising quality criteria enables everyone to get to the same place quickly and understand how judgement is being made by the PMO. When the PMO ensures that quality criteria is also backed up by industry standard and best practice, judgement can become more credible, respected, and compliance and adherence can then become easier for people.

Firstly, criteria needs to come from somewhere. The diagram below shows how criteria is generated.

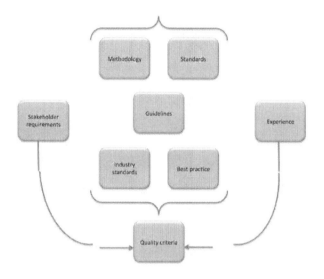

Some methodology and standards may not go into detail about what 'good' looks like. What is considered 'good' often varies between organisations, although industry standards and best practice can give an idea of what can be expected which can serve to be as fit for purpose as possible. However, generally (as an example) you usually won't find 'good' project plans in a Google search because as mentioned previously, it can be subjective from person to person and organisation to organisation.

It is therefore vital that a PMO defines, validates and sets quality criteria for evidence in audits and gate reviews with the help of key stakeholders if appropriate and required. This can be done in conjunction with a referral to existing specific departmental or corporate standards that may exist within an organisation, generic industry standard, generic best practice, stakeholder viewpoint, and personal experience to build criteria.

Even before criteria is put together, a list of documents and areas considered 'audit or gate review worthy' should be put together so that people know what it is the PMO is going to be looking at, and should be collated and published as part of the methodology.

Methodology in the project context, is the standard way (method) to go about managing a project. It should contain information about how a project should be broken down into portions (stages, gates and end of increment/ time box/ and sprint reviews) to make it less risky, easier to manage and to show the governance and processes to follow throughout the lifecycle to get things done, ensuring decisions can be obtained and made. It should also describe the people and departments to interact with and provide clarity around the templates and tools that are required to be filled in and documentation/task boards that should be produced as evidence of activity at various points.

As a PMO matures, so should its methodology or methodologies if there is more than one. When asking people to produce a document or to log something, whatever is produced should provide value and not waste time, or be a duplicate of something else. Something that is able to be consolidated into as fewer 'pieces of work' as possible not only makes the submitter's life easier but also makes the PMO's life easier by reviewing fewer documents whilst obtaining the same audit results.

The methodology is the starting point to create the list of items that indicates required evidence of project delivery as part of normal project activity, which then generates the ability to define quality criteria to enable audit and gate review based judgement.

It is not necessarily an easy task to get to a definition of quality for different documentational requirements, but once it is done and made publicly available, people can then be in no doubt as to what is expected of them and it makes it easy for the PMO team to know how to judge something.

In the course of defining a methodology, inevitably the required documentational evidence can also be determined. An example of building quality criteria, is that to say 'a project plan must be available at a certain point' is not enough. The PMO (in conjunction with key stakeholders if in any doubt) must define what it means to have a plan that is considered 'just enough to meet stakeholder needs'; whether that be criteria such as:

- Including all stage gates – in which case, what stage gates are required, or not required to be included?

- At what point in the delivery lifecycle should a plan be produced and what levels of detail are required at different points? Can further criteria be given (if appropriate) as to the size of the project and where it is in its lifecycle that determines the guideline amount of detail required?
- What governance, including decision making, review points and sign off, is required to be included?
- What tool the plan must be created in, if any? (i.e. is a spreadsheet acceptable? Using a tool such as Microsoft Project? Written down on a white board?)
- Dependencies must be included - in which case, a definition of a dependency and their types must be provided
- Should resource and cost information be included in the plan or be provided separately?

It is also useful to understand and communicate in the methodology exactly what needs to have quality criteria applied to it. In the first instance, where appropriate, it should be:

- The ability for project and programme managers to state which methodology is being used to manage projects and to adhere to that in supporting documentation.
- The ability for project and programme managers to know how to get initial and ongoing funding approval.
- The ability to state which stage gates the project will use to complete its lifecycle. Those stage gates should be in conjunction with a defined methodology (i.e. if the project is a small one and therefore only needs a superficial 'light touch' governance approach, this should explain why certain stage gates and

documentation will **NOT** be required or audit reviewed for the project).

- Defining quality criteria on each document or communication about project progress.
- How templates and tools should be filled in and used.
- Defining what it means to have completed the correct governance on a project throughout its lifecycle, including board compilation, board decision making, sponsor authority, gate review approvals by stakeholders and other subject matter experts, as well as go/no go decision making.
- What the approach is to auditing (determined through project prioritisation and assessment, or project sizing) and whether a full governance approach should be taken (i.e. a deep dive detailed look) or a superficial 'light touch' approach should be implemented. The definition between 'light touch' and 'full governance' should be made very clear.
- Storage of information; specifically, where to store it, what to store, how often to update it, who can access or see it, who can change it, when to delete it, and the implementation of version control.
- Defining when information should be provided both to the PMO (and other departments such as Finance) and what the PMO delivers.
- Definition of the role the PMO has at all levels, particularly in its assistance, support and information provision
- Definition of other roles and interfaces to and from the PMO and within the project community

Examples of methodology diagrams were given in my first book: 'Level up your PMO: 6 tips to make your PMO a success', and are shown below to indicate how projects are traditionally broken down in particular methodologies.

Stage suggestions for the waterfall, hybrid waterfall-agile and agile methodologies can be found in the diagrams below. Please note that these diagrams can be accessed at my website for free at the following location: http://www.pmosynergy.com/pmo-management---audit-x17592.html.

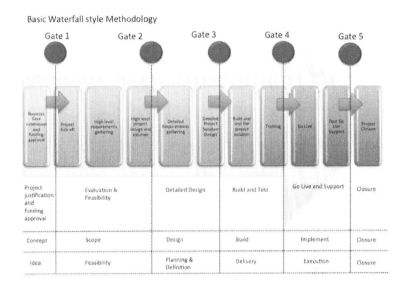

Basic Waterfall style Methodology

The diagram above represents a purely waterfall style methodology; underneath the coloured blocks there are three lines of different suggestions for stage gate names.

Basic Waterfall/Agile Hybrid Methodology

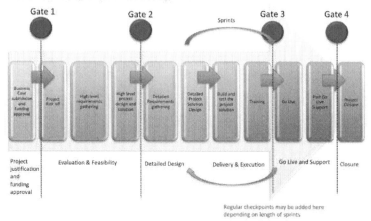

The diagram above represents agile elements integrated with waterfall in a 'hybrid waterfall-agile' type methodology as it is sometimes known, and common for organisations that run projects with both methodologies simultaneously. These usually exist because either the organisation prefers to retain the waterfall element to some degree, or that the organisation is using this method in the interim transitory period of maturity for pure agile.

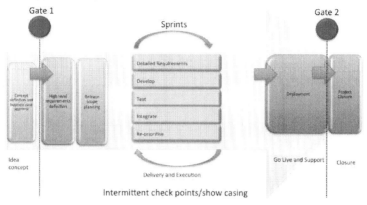

The diagram above represents a suggested purely agile methodology. Some may even suggest that the above is still a hybrid version of agile but organisations usually require PMO's to implement defined review points in the form of showcasing to check progress, risk and continued or ongoing value and justification.

Having a defined methodology also includes incorporating defined artefacts and documentation which are required to be created during each stage. These documents are used as evidence that specific activity has taken place in projects during audits and the quality gate review process.

The basic suggested checklist for the waterfall methodology is shown below (these diagrams can be accessed for free on my website at the following location: http://www.pmosynergy.com/pmo-management---audit-x17592.html).

35

Basic Waterfall Documentation Checklist at the end of key project stages

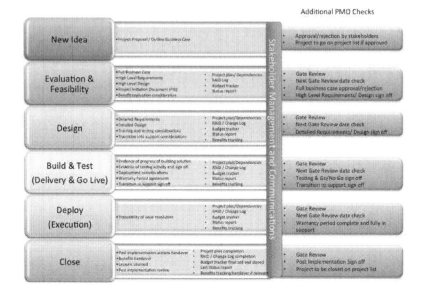

The checklist for the Agile methodology is as follows:

Basic Pure Agile Documentation Checklist at the end of key project stages

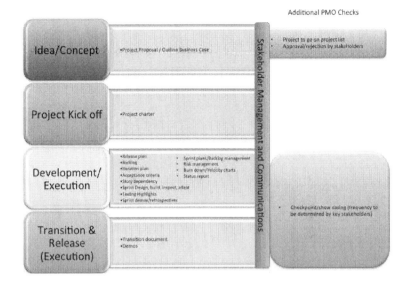

It is in this way that methodology can be used to generate the list of evidence required as part of normal project delivery activity, which can then be a starting point for creating quality criteria which enables audit and gate review based judgement.

Once a list has been obtained, the quality criteria can then be formed. Below is an example list of the documentation you might come across or use within your methodology and a checklist of accompanying questions which may be used as a guide in building good quality documentation and making them audit and gate review ready.

Criteria may exist below that pertain to different levels of PMO (for example, some questions may be purely portfolio or programme related), but can be tailored according to the level you might have in your organisation. The list below does not contain every single detailed template that might be found in the project lifecycle and there may be more documents that may need to be assessed but the list does contain a key selection that may be found at a fundamental level. Each organisation needs to be taken on a case by case basis, and as always, collaboration with key stakeholders is key to ensure that they are getting the assurance they need from the PMO and that the PMO is focussing on the right areas.

Outline Business case, project proposal, brief or charter

What is it? The title and contents of this document vary between methodology and organisation and may contain an outline scope, objectives, terms of reference and justification of the project that is usually used to secure further funding (and/or approval to continue).

Where would you find this in the lifecycle? At the very beginning of the project lifecycle, when justification for initial funding, stakeholder interest and approval to begin investigations are required.

Checklist of criteria and questions to ask in an audit or review:

Basic Hygiene Questions: Assuming there is a PMO or corporate template that people can populate, is all information that is required to be in this document present? Is the submitter using the correct and latest version? Is the spelling and grammar checked? If it refers to people, are the names and titles correct? If it refers to governance structure, it is correct? Has it been stored in the right location? Has it been submitted on time?

Criteria 1: Define as a standard whether it is important for the change outlined to be strategically aligned and prioritised or not, who should assess it and whether approval is required. Understand whether this piece of work has been or will be considered with or in any future plans for delivery. The

Portfolio Management function, if one exists, may seek to answer this question if it is important to the organisation. If not, does it matter? Has special dispensation been given for whatever reason? Is that dispensation written down anywhere?

Criteria 2: Does the organisation log, measure and track benefits? If so, is there a standard to assess against? How detailed does it have to be? What template do people need to use? Is the template filled in correctly? Are the benefits set out and clear?

Can an impact assessment of benefits within the overall existing programme or portfolio be made, if appropriate? How might this fit in to the list of projects (if part of a programme or portfolio) from a priority and strategic alignment perspective?

Criteria 3: Does the document generally 'make sense' to an outsider or someone not close to the project (i.e. you, the PMO)?

Criteria 4: Assuming a standard exists for risk management to assess against, are there any initial risks listed, highlighted or captured correctly (or can they be identified?) Are there any risks relating to its potential size and any impact to other live projects that are running? If assumptions are made, have they been validated as far as they can be? Might there be any dependency risk with any other live or potential project?

Criteria 5: Assess and analyse the impact of this piece of work to other existing projects (e.g. resource conflicts, resource capacity or dependency issues, delivery collision/timing). Are there any risks or issues?

Criteria 6: Are there any existing standards with regards to dealing with third party suppliers? If so, analyse the piece of work against those - are there any commercially related risks that might not have been identified?

Criteria 7: Scan the horizon, both in the local project or programme environment, other dependent projects or programmes, the external environment, or other departments; has any other legal, regulatory, technical, environmental, strategic, economic, financial, organisational, management, human, commercial, political, operational or infrastructure related impact been considered?

Full Business Case

What is it? This is a full version of the justification of the project, which is usually used to secure complete funding (and/or approval to fully start the project). Note that some of the criteria for the full business case might be similar to the outline business case because one document is a more advanced and populated version of the other according to the amount of information available at particular points.

Where would you find this in the lifecycle? This document is created just before the project starts in order to justify more investment. As it outlines fixed objectives such as time, cost and (depending on whether it is an agile project or not, scope) and because it is an evolving and live document, it should be updated after the project is re-baselined following initial creation after a change occurs to outline what those changes are. It should also show if there will be any change to the expected benefits.

Checklist of criteria and questions to ask in an audit or review:

Basic Hygiene Questions: Assuming there is a PMO or corporate template that people can populate, is all information that is required to be in this document present? Is the submitter using the correct and latest version? Is the spelling and grammar checked? If it refers to people, are the names and titles correct? If it refers to governance structure, it is correct? Has it been stored in the right location? Has it been submitted on time? Does it need to go through any other levels of approval?

Criteria 1: Does the business case fully articulate the justification for the project and clearly outline costs and benefits? Have the benefits been fully considered and identified?

Criteria 2: Does the organisation log, measure and track benefits? If so, is there a standard to assess against? How detailed does it have to be? What template do people need to use? Is the template filled in correctly?

Can an impact assessment of benefits within the overall existing programme or portfolio be made, if appropriate? How might this fit in to the list of projects (if part of a programme or portfolio) from a priority and strategic alignment perspective?

Criteria 3: Define as a standard whether it is important for the change outlined to be strategically aligned and prioritised or not, who should assess it and whether approval is required. The Portfolio Management function, if one exists, may seek to answer this question if it is important to the organisation. If not, does it matter? Has special dispensation been given for whatever reason? Is that dispensation written down anywhere?

Criteria 4: Has this piece of work been 'sized' (e.g. small, medium or large) through prioritisation and project assessment techniques and what impact might this have on other projects, programmes or the portfolio if appropriate?

Criteria 5: Does the business case make sense to an outsider and is it to the required level of quality required for something of its size? (i.e. depending on the organisational requirement, it may require more detail and more than just a couple of pages for something very large, risky or complex).

Criteria 6: If there has been a change or update to the business case, is the document fully updated, any additional funds tracked, approved and signed off by all relevant approvers and stakeholders according to governance requirements?

Criteria 7: Assuming a standard exists for risk management to assess against, are there any initial risks listed, highlighted or captured correctly (or can they be identified?) Are there any risks relating to its potential size and any other live projects that are running? If assumptions are made, have they been validated as far as they can be? Might there be any dependency risk with any other live or potential project?

Criteria 8: Assess and analyse the impact of this piece of work to other existing projects (e.g. resource conflicts, resource capacity or dependency issues, delivery collision/timing). Are there any risks or issues?

Criteria 9: Are there any existing standards with regards to dealing with third party suppliers? If so, analyse the piece of work against those - are there any commercially related risks that might not have been identified?

Criteria 10: Scan the horizon, both in the local project or programme environment, other dependent projects or programmes, the external environment, or other departments; has any other legal, regulatory, technical, environmental, strategic, economic, financial, organisational, management, human, commercial, political, operational or infrastructure related impact been considered?

Criteria 11: If reviewing the business case after initial approval, has any elements to the project during the lifecycle been updated or changed, and are these changes reflected in the business case as an update? Are they also reflected in the matching documentation – for example, has a change been logged (if appropriate) and have the financials been adjusted?

Documentation that contains requirements

What is it? This is the list of needs (and wants) of project stakeholders that forms the foundations for delivery of the project. These will be high level initially to obtain high level estimates before going into detail once the funding has been approved. It will depend on the methodology being used as to how detailed the requirements are at a particular time in the lifecycle, but also how they are presented.

Where would you find this in the lifecycle? High-level requirements are usually generated in the very early stages of a project and then further defined and developed as the project progresses, if it is approved to continue.

Checklist of criteria and questions to ask in an audit or review:

Hygiene Questions: Are there any business analysis, departmental or corporate standards that should be followed in terms of physical presentation of this information? Assuming there is a template that people can populate, is all information that is required to be in this document present? Is the submitter using the correct and latest version? Is the spelling and grammar checked? If it refers to people, are the names and titles correct? If it refers to governance or any other organisational structure, it is correct? Has it been stored in the right location? Has it been submitted on time? Does it need to go through any other levels of approval?

Criteria 1: If appropriate for the PMO, it can perform a high level review of the requirements as far as knowledge in the team goes in relation to the entire project, its objectives, and its stakeholders. Bear in mind that the PMO may not have the subject matter knowledge to fully understand the requirements, but this does not stop the PMO from reviewing documentation and seeing whether there are gaps or problems with cross matching in documentation across the project which may reveal potential impacts, risks or issues. If any risks or issues are identified, are they captured?

Criteria 2: Check that any requirements documentation has the relevant level of detail relative to the size of the initiative and that it makes sense to the generic reader. It is also good for the PMO to obtain a high level knowledge of what is being delivered so that this can be retained later on in the project in terms of the plan, risks or issues, and for supporting any other documentation (e.g. architectural and design documentation).

Criteria 3: Has the requirements been reviewed and signed off by all relevant approvers according to governance requirements?

Documentation that contains the design of the solution

What is it? This is the composition, depiction or architecture of what is going to be delivered. For example, if a house were to be built, this would be the blueprint showing how it should be built along with how it all fits together. This usually is delivered at a high level initially in order to obtain high level estimates before going into detail once funding has been approved.

Where would you find this in the lifecycle? The high level (outline) design of the solution is usually generated when it is still being determined as to whether the project is viable or not, and then further developed at the detailed level if the project is approved to continue. In waterfall projects, it is usually completed after the requirements have been approved and signed off and just before work begins on building the solution. In agile projects, the design is known at a high level first, and then further detail is determined during each time box or sprint.

Checklist of criteria and questions to ask in an audit or review:

Hygiene Questions: Are there any architectural, corporate or departmental standards that should be followed in terms of physical presentation of this information? Assuming there is a template that people can populate, is all information that is required to be in this document present? Is the submitter using the correct and latest version? Is the spelling and grammar checked? If it refers to people, are the names and titles correct? If it refers to governance or any other organisational structure, it is correct? Has it been stored in the right location? Has it been submitted on time? Does it need to go through any other levels of approval?

Criteria 1: If appropriate to the organisation, the PMO can perform a high level review of the design as far as knowledge in the team goes in relation to the entire project, its objectives, and its stakeholders. Bear in mind that the PMO may not have the subject matter knowledge to fully understand the design, but this does not stop the PMO from reviewing documentation and seeing whether there are gaps or problems with cross matching in documentation across the project which may reveal potential impacts, risks or issues. If any risks or issues are identified, are they captured?

Criteria 2: Have all relevant approvers, stakeholders, bodies or committees signed off the solution design according to governance requirements?

Criteria 3: Is there anything else the PMO should be checking according to any design authority?

Documentation that kicks the project off

What is it? This is a document that describes all the key elements of the project at a summary level of how the project is going to be managed and delivered, including summarised information about the business case. The name and contents of this document can vary depending on the methodology, and can sometimes be referred to as a 'PID' or 'project initiation document' in waterfall projects, or a 'management approach definition' or 'MAD' in APMG's agile project management.

Where would you find this in the lifecycle? This document would be created before the project actually starts once all key information is known about requirements, design and delivery approach. It remains a live and evolving document throughout the project and should be maintained and updated after every change to keep the summary current.

Checklist of criteria and questions to ask in an audit or review:

Hygiene Questions: Are there any PMO project kick off standards that should be followed in terms of physical presentation of this information? Assuming there is a template that people can populate, is all information that is required to be in this document present? Is the submitter using the correct and latest version? Is the spelling and grammar checked? If it refers to people, are the names and titles correct? If it refers to governance or any other organisational structure, it is correct? Has it been stored in the right location? Has it been submitted on time? Does it need to go through any other levels of approval or review?

Criteria 1: Does the document generally 'make sense' to an outsider or someone not close to the project (i.e. you, the PMO)?

Criteria 2: Does the contents of the document align and match with data in other documents (e.g. plans, business case, requirements, design, risk and issue logs)?

Criteria 3: Does the funding details match what was approved in the original business case?

Criteria 4: Does the allocation of resource and time to do certain activities look correct? (For example, does the amount of days and resource allocated to particular activities look adequate considering the size of the project?) This question can be answered more over time with evidence based estimating, which means using the data gathered from the past to predict the future.

Criteria 5: Does the outline plan and timescales in this document match the actual project plan and what was originally stated in the business case?

Criteria 6: Assuming a standard exists for risk and issue management, are key risks and issues identified and captured in this document and in any other appropriate places (e.g. the RAID log)? If there are newly identified actual or potential risks by the PMO, this needs to be raised with the Project

Manager or other relevant person who should ensure those are logged and maintained.

Criteria 7: Are there any dependencies (in this project, other projects, the Programme or the Portfolio as a whole if that is relevant) that may need to be taken into consideration? Is there any associated risk in that sense?

Criteria 8: Is this document an accurate picture of what has happened so far and what is going to happen, and does it contain adequate enough detail that gives a full summary of all the key elements for the project?

Criteria 9: Is sponsor representation at an adequate level of seniority? Is there adequate sponsor commitment in place?

Criteria 10: Have all relevant approvers, stakeholders, bodies or committees signed off the document according to governance requirements?

Planning documentation

What is it? Planning involves the integration of many different elements of the project into one overall place in order that activity can be tracked as far into the future as feasibly possible with known information. Planning is the outward evidence that activity is and is going to happen, and is often created as a personal project checklist, but also to reassure stakeholders about what is going to happen in terms of delivery when translated to a higher level. The overall plan may include a schedule for the project, cost allocation against activity, key documentation creation, benefits, gate and other governance review points, stakeholder engagement planning, communication planning, and resource allocation against activity.

Where would you find this in the lifecycle? Plans are normally created as soon as information is known about the future, whether that be in the next day, the next week, few weeks, months or years. A plan is normally required to help stakeholders understand what is going to happen at least to the next stage of a project if other activity further out is not known. As soon as that activity is known, it should be populated into the plan. Plans should be further refined, defined and developed as time goes on when more detail is known.

Checklist of criteria and questions to ask in an audit or review:

Hygiene Questions: Assuming PMO planning standards exist, are they being followed in terms of physical presentation of this information? Assuming there is a template that people can populate, is all information that is required to be in this document at this point present? Is the submitter applying correct version control? If it refers to people, are the names and titles correct? If it refers to governance or any other organisational structure, it is correct? Has it been stored in the right location? Does it need to go through any other levels of approval or review?

Criteria 1: Does the plan or plans generally 'make sense' to an outsider or someone not close to the project (i.e. you, the PMO)?

Criteria 2: Does the contents of the plan align and match with data in other documents (e.g. business case, kick off documents, reports, requirements, design, third party documents etc.)?

Criteria 3: Do costs, if part of the plan, match what was approved in the original business case?

Criteria 4: Does the allocation of resource and time to do certain activities look correct? (For example, does the amount of days and resource allocated to particular activities look adequate considering the size of the project?) This question can be answered more over time with evidence based estimating, which means using the data gathered from the past to predict the future.

Criteria 5: Does the plan and timescales in this document match what was originally stated in the business case?

Criteria 6: Does the plan contain enough expected detail relative to the size and complexity of the project?

Criteria 7: Does the plan contain all (standard and non standard) key milestones and are all gates planned in?

Criteria 8: Does the plan have key activity and its detail planned in (e.g. building the solution and testing the solution as well as deployment activity and what will happen during the warranty period?)

Criteria 9: Where relevant, have plans been baselined, or re-baselined? Is it noted down what the re-baseline objectives are and is there cross-matching documentation to support it (e.g. change requests)?

Criteria 10: Have critical path tasks been identified?

Criteria 11: Have dependencies (in this project, other projects, the Programme or the Portfolio as a whole if that is relevant) been identified and captured? Is there any associated risk in that sense?

Criteria 12: If part of a programme or portfolio, does the plan have any other impact to those or other projects?

Criteria 13: How frequently is the plan being updated? Is that in line with the update frequency requirements by the department?

Criteria 14: Assuming a standard exists for risk and issue management, are plan related risks and issues identified and captured and in any other appropriate places (e.g. the RAID log)? If there are newly identified actual or potential risks by the PMO, this needs to be raised with the Project Manager or other relevant person who should ensure those are logged and maintained.

Resourcing Documentation

What is it? Resourcing in this context refers to the allocation, control, acquisition and demobilisation of people to and from projects and is symbiotic with the planning and project controls processes. It can mean the act of balancing and understanding the capacity of individuals to do one or many projects, and the capacity of the department and teams versus what is needed in future project demand.

Where would you find this in the lifecycle? Resourcing is required at all points in the project lifecycle. Where things need to be done, resources will be required. Resourcing plans may go hand in hand with the project schedule plan or it may be contained within a separate document or tool.

Checklist of criteria and questions to ask in an audit or review:

Hygiene Questions: Assuming PMO resourcing standards exist, are they being followed in terms of physical presentation of this information? Assuming there is a template that people can populate, is all information that is required to be in this document at this point present? Is the submitter applying correct version control? If it refers to people, are the names and titles correct? If it refers to governance or any other organisational structure, it is correct? Has it been stored in the right location? Does it need to go through any other levels of approval or review?

Criteria 1: Does the resource plan 'make sense' to an outsider or someone not close to the project (i.e. you, the

PMO)?

Criteria 2: Are all resources that are known to be being used on the project, listed in any related project plan/documentation or tool? Is it clear what their capacity and utilisation is? Is it clear how resources are spread across multiple projects (if relevant) and is it clear how much availability resources have left?

Criteria 3: Is it clear when resources start and finish on the project?

Criteria 4: Is planned leave made clear?

Criteria 5: How frequently is the resourcing plan being updated? Is that in line with the update frequency requirements by the department?

Criteria 6: Is it clear how long resources have been secured for from start to finish in the project?

Criteria 7: Is it known when contract or temporary resource end/renewal dates are?

Criteria 8: If coming towards the end of a project, is it clear what will happen to resources once they have been stood down off this particular project?

Criteria 9: If relevant, is it clear how third party contractors and consultants should be utilised and controlled from a resourcing perspective within this project?

Criteria 10: Assuming a standard exists for risk and issue management, are resourcing related risks and issues identified and captured in this document and in any other appropriate places (e.g. the RAID log)? If there are newly identified actual or potential risks by the PMO, this needs to be raised with the Project Manager or other relevant person who should ensure those are logged and maintained.

Financial Documentation

What is it? Financial documentation contains the costs/budget for the project. Some organisations also require financial benefits, the expected return on investment and net present value of the project to be included also.

The document might be known as a 'financial appraisal', or a 'finance tracker' and costs can be detailed either in spreadsheets, or relevant tools such as finance systems or project management tools.

Where would you find this in the lifecycle? Costs should be considered right up front from early inception of an idea and monitored and tracked right the way through. If more budget is assigned for whatever reason, this should also be noted, added to the overall 'pot' and tracked. Costs and budget are considered to be a key control and is one of the main drivers for projects.

Checklist of criteria and questions to ask in an audit or review:

Hygiene Questions: Assuming PMO, Finance department, or corporate financial standards exist, are they being followed in terms of physical presentation of this information? Assuming there is a template that people can populate, is all information that is required to be in this document at this point present? Is the submitter applying correct version control? If it refers to people, are the names and titles correct? If costs are categorised, are the categories correct? Has it been stored in the right location? Does financial documentation need to go through any other levels of approval or review?

Criteria 1: Does the financial plan 'make sense' to an outsider or someone not close to the project (i.e. you, the PMO)?

Criteria 2: Is it clear whether the funds have been fully approved or not?

Criteria 3: Have the costs been allocated and forecasted correctly month by month?

Criteria 4: Is it showing a correct variance in terms of an under or over spend?

Criteria 5: Are resource costs correct (in terms of contractor or blended rates)?

Criteria 6: Has third party and supplier costs been correctly captured?

Criteria 7: Is the document or tool being updated as frequently as the department requires?

Criteria 8: Are actual costs being reconciled each month?

Criteria 9: Does the information cross match across other documentation including plans, the business case, and reports?

Criteria 10: Has any appropriate adjustment been made in terms of currency (if relevant)?

Criteria 11: Is it clear what the burn or run rate is of costs per month? Does this add up in terms of the total cost of the project?

Criteria 12: Is there anything else to consider (e.g. availability of budget or cost allocation) in terms of projects operating across financial years?

Criteria 13: If the project is being funded by stage, is this clearly articulated in terms of any documentation?

Criteria 14: Assuming a standard exists for risk and issue management, are financial risks and issues identified and captured in this document and in any other appropriate places (e.g. the RAID log)? If there are newly identified actual or potential risks by the PMO, this needs to be raised with the Project Manager or other relevant person who should ensure those are logged and maintained.

Criteria 15: Are changes that require additional budget clearly logged and is any newly approved budget documented?

Criteria 16: If required, does the document or tool correctly show return on investment (ROI) or net present value (NPV)?

Criteria 17: Is it clear and documented as to where the funds have come from, when the funds were approved and by whom?

Procurement and Commercial documentation

What is it? Procurement and commercial documentation, processes and tools can be anything relating to the buying of goods and services from third parties and any contracts associated with that.

Where would you find this in the lifecycle? As soon as the project knows it needs to buy something, it will need to follow the commercial and procurement processes of the organisation (if they have them). This will involve ensuring that any contracts and milestone plans are in place before work commences and that lead times (how long it takes between the order of something and the delivery of something) for delivery of goods are known so that co-ordination of what needs to happen can occur.

Checklist of criteria and questions to ask in an audit or review:

Hygiene Questions: Assuming procurement department, supplier management, departmental or corporate standards exist, are they being followed in terms of physical presentation of this information? Assuming there is a template that people can populate, is all information that is required to be in this document at this point present? Is the submitter applying correct version control? If it refers to people, are the names and titles correct? If costs are categorised, are the categories correct? Has it been stored in the right location? Does this documentation need to go through any other levels of approval or review?

Criteria 1: If appropriate for the PMO, it can perform a high level review of the procurement and commercial documentation as far as knowledge in the team goes in relation to the entire project, its objectives, and its stakeholders. Bear in mind that the PMO may not have the subject matter knowledge to fully understand it, but this does not stop the PMO from reviewing it and seeing whether there are gaps or problems with cross matching in documentation across the project which may reveal potential impacts, risks or issues. If any risks or issues are identified, are they captured?

Criteria 2: Does any procurement and commercial documentation 'make sense' to an outsider or someone not close to the project (i.e. you, the PMO)?

Criteria 3: Assuming a standard exists for risk and issue management, are procurement and commercial related risks and issues identified and captured in this document and in any other appropriate places (e.g. the RAID log)? If there are newly identified actual or potential risks by the PMO, this needs to be raised with the Project Manager or other relevant person who should ensure those are logged and maintained.

Criteria 4: Is key information in procurement or commercial documentation cross matched and captured across other documents (e.g. the project schedule, financial tracker etc.…)?

Criteria 5: If there is key activity or payment at a milestone, is this captured and are the reviews for this planned in?

Criteria 6: Are lead times for delivery clear, written down and any risks identified and mitigated?

Criteria 7: With the advice of the relevant department, are the correct contracts in place at the right time?

Criteria 8: At the relevant point in the lifecycle, if there are issues with suppliers or third parties, are these being dealt with effectively?

Criteria 9: If in place, are the tools and processes around this subject being utilised and followed correctly?

Criteria 10: Are there any procurement related or commercial dependencies (in this project, other projects, the Programme or the Portfolio as a whole if that is relevant) that may need to be taken into consideration? Is there any associated risk in that sense?

Criteria 11: Has the requirements been reviewed and signed off by all relevant approvers according to governance requirements?

Controls

What are they? Project controls are ways to track, manage and monitor elements of the project that may threaten the delivery of its objectives. By implementing project control techniques, there is a greater chance of delivery success and to decrease failure. Control techniques[2] can include:

- Risk management
- Issue management
- Scope and Change management
- Stakeholder and communication management
- Gate reviews

Where would you find this in the lifecycle? Risk and issue management should be employed as soon as any are detected and can normally be identified fairly early on. Scope and change control should be employed as soon as the project is baselined. Stakeholder and communication management should be started as soon as the project begins. Gate reviews are planned in at predefined points according to the methodology (if there is one). All of these control techniques once started should be tracked, managed and monitored all the way through the project until it closes.

Checklist of criteria and questions to ask in an audit or review:

---

[2] A definition of control techniques can be found in the glossary

Hygiene Questions: Assuming control standards exist, are they being followed in terms of physical presentation of this information? Assuming there is a template that people can populate, is all information that is required to be in this document at this point present? Is the submitter applying correct version control? If it refers to people, are the names and titles correct? If it refers to governance or any other organisational structure, it is correct? Has it been stored in the right location? Does it need to go through any other levels of approval or review?

Criteria 1: Does control documentation and the contents 'make sense' to an outsider or someone not close to the project (i.e. you, the PMO)?

Criteria 2: Assuming a standard exists for risk and issue management, are risks and issues identified and captured in the correct way, with the required quality and in appropriate places (e.g. the RAID log)? If there are newly identified actual or potential risks by the PMO, this needs to be raised with the Project Manager or other relevant person who should ensure those are logged and maintained. Use the following risk categories to check whether there is anything that may not have been identified:

- Strategic risk
- Commercial risk
- Financial risk
- Economic risk
- Organisational risk
- Management risk
- Human resources risk
- Political risk
- Environmental risk

- Technical risk
- Operational risk
- Infrastructure risk

Criteria 3: Are risks and issues scored correctly, and does it have the correct RAG assigned to it?

Criteria 4: Can any risks or issues be aggregated to form a different level of risk (i.e. forming different risk at the project level or aggregated risk at a programme, portfolio, departmental or corporate level)?

Criteria 5: Do all risks and issues have owners, and are they being updated within the required frequency?

Criteria 6: Do all risks contain appropriate mitigating actions and issues contain appropriate resolution procedures?

Criteria 7: If a risk has turned into an issue, is this documented and cross-referenced correctly?

Criteria 8: Is it clear what is in scope and what is out of scope, and are changes adequately represented through the change management process?

Criteria 9: Does the scope match the requirements?

Criteria 10: Assuming there is a PMO standard in place for change control, are changes that are raised logged correctly and is it to the required level of quality (i.e. it adequately describes what is being changed, how long it will take, how much it will cost, what the impact is or will be etc.)?

Criteria 11: Are changes going through the correct and appropriate governance channels for approval?

Criteria 12: Are budgets and timelines being adjusted and plans rebaselined following a change?

Criteria 13: If any changes occurred as a result of an issue, has the relevant updates been made to both the change and the issue?

Criteria 14: Assuming a tolerance level is set, is the project adhering to those?

Criteria 15: Assuming there are PMO standards in place for stakeholder and communication management, is it made clear in relevant documentation what the project intends to do around stakeholder engagement, management and communication? Are there stakeholder 'heat maps' in place (if appropriate or relevant)? Is communication and engagement mechanisms clear? Are meetings planned out? Are there stakeholder survey's in place to indicate project satisfaction levels (if appropriate or relevant)? Is there any feedback or stakeholder insight that the PMO knows about that they can tell the project or programme manager?

Criteria 16: Assuming a defined methodology exists, are gate reviews planned in?

Criteria 17: Assuming a documentation checklist exists, is the project manager ready for each gate review? Is there anything the PMO can learn from in terms of what people are or are not doing to improve the methodology?

Criteria 18: Have the relevant authorities signed off or provided approval at the required points?

Reporting

What is it? Status and dashboard reporting are ways to display summary and key information about a project that can show key stakeholders positive and negative progress in a project. It can come in many formats, and can be pictorial or purely text. It can also be required in different frequencies ranging from every day, to every week, month, or quarter depending on the purpose of the report and information needed.

Where would you find this in the lifecycle? Overall project status reports should be created as soon as feasibly possible and as soon as information starts to be known, and then reproduced at the required frequency thereafter until the project closes. A standard should be in place as to when reports are to first be expected after the project manager starts on the project. Usually my recommendation is to start after a two week period.

Checklist of criteria and questions to ask in an audit or review:

Hygiene Questions: Assuming PMO reporting standards exist, are they being followed in terms of physical presentation of this information? Assuming there is a template that people can populate, is all information that is required to be in this document at this point present? Is the submitter applying correct version control and correct dates? If it refers to people, are the names and titles correct? If it refers to governance or any other organisational structure, it is correct? Has it been stored in the right location? Does it need to go through any other levels of approval or review?

Criteria 1: Does the report 'make sense' to an outsider or someone not close to the project (i.e. you, the PMO)?

Criteria 2: Does the report contain the correct name of the Project or Programme Manager, correct date, correct lifecycle stage, correct project name or unique project identifier?

Criteria 3: Is the executive summary adequate? Does it say enough for anyone not close to the project to know what is going on? Is there any information in the executive summary that can be used to determine whether there is accuracy (or not) elsewhere in the report (e.g. risks, issues, the plan, overall RAG's etc.)?

Criteria 4: Is the activity in this period or next period (if those are fields in the report) adequate, and does it say enough for anyone not close to the project to know what is going on? Is there any information in these fields that can be used to determine whether there is accuracy (or not) elsewhere in the report (e.g. risks, issues, the plan, overall RAG's etc.)?

Criteria 5: Does the summary schedule look correct? If appropriate or relevant, is it baselined and does it correctly show current progress against the baseline? Do key milestones and stage gate review dates match what is in the plan? Are there any gaps or blanks in dates and is there a good reason why? If milestones are labelled with a RAG assessment, does it look consistent and is there anything to indicate any risk (Amber) or an issue (red)? Is the lifecycle stage the project is currently in correct and are past milestones labelled as complete? Are dependencies flagged (if relevant)?

Criteria 6: Do the risks and issues make sense and are they reflective of what is going on in the other project summaries (and cross matched to the risk and issue logs)? Are they written with enough detail? Are risks written as risks and issues written as issues? If there are, for example, red risks or issues, yet the project is reporting an overall green, there needs to be an explanation for this.

Criteria 7: Is there anything that the PMO knows about the project which should be captured in the report but isn't? Is there anything that the PMO should escalate (to the report owner in the first instance)?

Criteria 8: Does any budget information match and accurately summarise any other financial documentation?

Benefits Realisation considerations

What is it? This may include information populated into a benefits log or tracker and a benefits realisation plan that provides a way of summarising, tracking, managing and maintaining those benefits on behalf of the business/sponsor. There may also be information about benefits 'owners' and what their roles and responsibilities are.

Where would you find this in the lifecycle? This would be created once the benefits start to be identified, usually when a project idea starts to develop in the very early stages, and then considered at every stage gate or time box review thereafter. The Project Manager 'looks after' the tracking and monitoring of the benefits as soon as the business case is approved on behalf of the business, reporting the progress for benefits realisation on a regular basis until the project goes live and closes, and then the benefits are handed back to the sponsor or a suitable business representative to manage and monitor if the benefits are not realised at that point.

Checklist of criteria and questions to ask in an audit or review:

Hygiene Questions: Are there any PMO benefits related standards that should be followed in terms of physical presentation of this information? Assuming there is a template that people can populate, is all information that is required to be in this document present? Is the submitter using the correct and latest version? Is the spelling and grammar checked? If it refers to people, are the names and titles correct? If it refers to governance or any other organisational structure, it is correct? Has it been stored in the right location? How often is it required to be updated and is that being done? Does it need to go through any other levels of approval or review from any other party and is there evidence that those people have seen it (e.g. the business)?

Criteria 1: Determine whether a separate benefits realisation plan is required (to the main project plan) and in what format and template. Does the plan articulate benefits and when they should be realised as well as review points throughout the project or programme lifecycle? Does it articulate the stakeholders and benefits owners that will be involved, and will there be any approvals required? If so, when are those approvals required?

Criteria 2: Determine whether logs and trackers are required and in what format and template. Does the log articulate and match the benefits as stated in the original business case? Are there any changes that might suggest a gap, a risk or an issue?

Criteria 3: If there are any changes to original project objectives later on, has the log, the business case and any other evolutionary and relevant document also been updated?

Criteria 4: Is there evidence that benefits review meetings are taking place (in terms of the plan, meeting minutes or any other form)? Is there evidence of stakeholder feelings around project delivery, progress or success up to that point and is there anything the PMO can help or assist with in this sense?

Criteria 5: Is there a standard in place for the updating of benefits realisation during the lifecycle? If so, are benefits being actively monitored and adhering to those standards?

Assessing quality assessment procedures (such as testing)

What is it? Quality assessment procedures are ways of reviewing and proving the fitness for purpose of something in a project, through the use of functions and processes such as testing and auditing.

Where would you find this in the lifecycle? Quality assessment procedures should be considered during the initial stages of a project, particularly when building the design of the solution, and reviewed regularly thereafter with an expectation that the solution that is built will have some final assessment to make sure it is satisfactory and sufficient according to original user requirement and is ready to 'go live'.

Checklist of criteria and questions to ask in an audit or review:

Hygiene Questions: Are there any PMO or other QA standards that should be followed in terms of physical presentation of this information or the processes that should be followed? Assuming there are templates that people can populate, is all information that is required present? Is the submitter using the correct and latest version? Is the spelling and grammar checked? If it refers to people, are the names and titles correct? If it refers to governance or any other organisational structure, it is correct? Has it been stored in the right location? How often is it required to be updated and is that being done? Does it need to go through any other levels of approval or review from any other party and is there evidence that those people have seen it (e.g. a testing or quality assurance function at a local, departmental or corporate level)?

Criteria 1: If appropriate to the organisation, the PMO can perform a high level review of what is presented as far as knowledge in the team goes in relation to the entire project, its objectives, and its stakeholders. Bear in mind that the PMO may not have the subject matter knowledge to fully understand it, but this does not stop the PMO from reviewing and seeing whether there are gaps or problems with cross matching in documentation across the project which may reveal potential impacts, risks or issues. If any risks or issues are identified, are they captured?

Criteria 2: Are there any quality or testing strategies in place that can be referred to when reviewing documentation? There may be industry specific documentation, test cases, user cases and defect resolution evidence that the PMO can look at to see what has been completed.

Criteria 3: Where possible, cross-match the information available to the main project plan (the quality management or testing plan may be integrated into the main plan) and ensure the details match and make sense, and ensure that it looks feasible for the timescales stated. This may be something the PMO can do more over time with evidence based estimating, which means using the data gathered from the past to predict or understand what looks suitable in future.

Criteria 4: Look for evidence of the value of project results (e.g. Customer satisfaction surveys, stakeholder opinion, and post implementation or time box review) to assess whether there is satisfaction with the product or the level of quality being achieved.

Criteria 5: Where testing is involved, look for successful test results with a low error or defect rate, or successful or swift resolution to errors and defects.

Criteria 6: Understand before the project begins whether compliance is needed for regulatory or organisational policy. At the appropriate times during the project, look for evidence of conformance to those policies or requirements.

Criteria 7: Have all relevant approvers, stakeholders, bodies or committees signed off the relevant items according to governance requirements?

Training Considerations

What is it? Training is a way to ensure that the end user understands the solution and how to use it once it goes live, either through (but not limited to) classroom based training, user testing, documentation and training manuals, quick reference cards or guides, user review, and computer based training.

Where would you find this in the lifecycle? Training is considered in the early stages of the project, particularly when designing the solution and reviewed thereafter with a PMO review point just before go-live so that there are no surprises and everyone involved has the necessary confidence in what they need to do or know. Training considerations may be completed by the Project Manager, a specialist person/team/function or a (people) change management function.

Checklist of criteria and questions to ask in an audit or review:

Hygiene Questions: Are there any PMO or other training standards that should be followed in terms of physical presentation of this information or the processes that should be followed? Assuming there are templates that people can populate, is all information that is required present? Is the submitter using the correct and latest version? Is the spelling and grammar checked? If it refers to people, are the names and titles correct? If it refers to governance or any other organisational structure, it is correct? Has it been stored in the right location? Does it need to go through any other levels of approval or review from any other party and is there evidence that those people have seen it?

Criteria 1: The PMO should look for evidence that training has or is being considered at the relevant points and that stakeholders are content or comfortable with the approach. The approach, where appropriate, should be clear and laid out so that people understand in advance what is going to happen at the relevant points.

Criteria 2: There may be evidence of training material which the PMO can review for its presence and fitness for purpose (as far as knowledge in the team goes) and ensure that training material is stored in the relevant place for future projects or people joining the organisation.

Criteria 3: Have all relevant approvers, stakeholders or departments signed off the relevant items according to governance requirements?

Documentation for transition into support and business as usual

What is it? This is the document or set of documents that best describe in detail how the transfer from project state to business as usual will be managed, by whom and what exactly needs to be done once the project goes live (including ongoing support and maintenance). It may describe in detail what happens in the moments before go-live to the moments after go-live (including any release, deployment, change or service management planning and procedures), as well as what happens 'post-implementation'. It may also include details of the warranty period; this is a certain agreed period of time where any faults or defects can be fixed by the project or any need for additional user support or coaching can be provided by the project before the project is accepted fully into 'business as usual'. The project is then able to close.

Where would you find this in the lifecycle? Transition into support elements should be considered during the early stages of the project, perhaps during the design of the solution and reviewed thereafter. A document or set of documents may be created which could include sets of instructions, designs and descriptions of the service that will be offered once the project goes live, release and deployment plans, service level or supplier agreements, people to contact during the transition and after go live until the end of the warranty period etc. This should be approved before the project goes live.

Be aware that warranty periods can be set by the PMO, department or organisation as a standard for projects but if using third party suppliers, they may also have their own warranty terms. The Project Manager is responsible for ensuring that whatever is agreed is made clear in any associated documentation so that people know what to expect once the project goes live.

Checklist of criteria and questions to ask in an audit or review:

Hygiene Questions: Are there any PMO or other transition into support standards that should be followed in terms of physical presentation of this information or the processes that should be followed? Assuming there are templates that people can populate, is all information that is required present? Is the submitter using the correct and latest version? Is the spelling and grammar checked? If it refers to people, are the names and titles correct? If it refers to governance or any other organisational structure, it is correct? Has it been stored in the right location? Does it need to go through any other levels of approval or review from any other party and is there evidence that those people have seen it?

Criteria 1: If appropriate to the organisation, the PMO can perform a high level review of what is presented as far as knowledge in the team goes in relation to the entire project, its objectives, and its stakeholders. Bear in mind that the PMO may not have the subject matter knowledge to fully understand all of it, but this does not stop the PMO from reviewing and seeing whether there are gaps or problems with cross matching in documentation across the project which may reveal potential impacts, risks or issues. If any risks or issues are identified, are they captured?

Criteria 2: The PMO should check that any deployment or release management planning type activity is reflected in the main project plan (if it is not already part of it).

Criteria 3: There may be different sets of governance requirements and approvers for different types of documentation and the PMO should make sure that these are adhered to at the relevant points throughout the lifecycle. Have all relevant approvers, stakeholders or departments signed off the relevant items according to governance requirements?

Criteria 4: Are lessons learned captured? Can these be aggregated at a Programme, Portfolio, departmental or Corporate level and taken forward for continuous improvement?

Criteria 5: Have any benefits been realised, or is there a plan to realise benefits over time after the project has closed? Has this been handed to the business?

Criteria 6: Are any risks, issues and changes closed off in the relevant places at the appropriate times?

Criteria 7: Is there proof that post implementation actions are going to be handed over to relevant parties and that there is clear ownership in place for those actions?

Criteria 8: Did the project achieve its original objectives and is that documented in a project closure report?

Criteria 9: Has the business and any other relevant stakeholders signed the project off as complete and closed once it gets to that point?

Criteria 10: Is service delivery happy to accept the project into support?

In Summary:

- In defining the methodology, the quality criteria for auditing can then be determined.

- A level of detail is necessary around quality criteria, as much as is required so that people generically know what is considered 'just enough' and that the PMO understand how judgement can be made on that.

- The PMO should keep an eye on lessons learned and stakeholder feedback to ensure that ongoing and appropriate (but not unnecessary) improvement can be made to the requirements and quality criteria on the production of evidence based documents, artefacts and any information delivered through any other means.

- The PMO must make sure that if in a PMO with more than one project, that project prioritisation, assessment and sizing is implemented as part of the methodology to determine what the governance and auditing priorities are.

- Each piece of evidence will require examination and how this happens will vary from organisation to organisation. It is important to understand what the organisational, departmental and stakeholder specific requirements are, as well as taking into account what already exists within an organisation to form what is required to examine documentation and any other evidence in audits and gate reviews.

Chapter 3

Scoring quality in an audit

· ·

Before undertaking an audit, all PMO members involved
need to understand and apply the quantifiable and visual
measurement that indicates levels of audit success. This may
differ between PMO's with different objectives and the
importance placed on areas may vary between organisations.

The guide below has been put together to help determine a
basic scoring mechanism for quality, based on the fact that
quality criteria has already been defined. It is crucial that
everyone involved in the audit (auditors and auditees) knows
what the criteria and measurements mean to avoid
misunderstandings or different levels of interpretation.

Quality Measure	Area Rating (RAG)	Description
Marginal (Non or low compliance)	0 or RED	There is no application of the process or procedures or adherence to the quality criteria. Questions could not be answered satisfactorily, or documentation was not available.
	1 or RED	There has been an attempt at

		application of the process or procedures but implementation has been ineffective and insufficient and shows marginal quality value.
	2 or AMBER	Partial application is in effect but results are still unsatisfactory and there is room for improvement.
	3 or AMBER	Fundamentals are in place, but not are fully implemented. Results are partially acceptable.
	4 or GREEN	There is satisfactory application of the process; it is broadly used and effectively maintained.
Superior (Full compliance)	5 or GREEN	Fully implemented and fully effective to the required level of quality. May exceed expectation. Data fully cross matches and processes are fully applied.

When talking about RAG in an audit (as detailed in the table above), red is similar to the RAG assessment in other project areas such as risk management and reporting. Red indicates troubled areas or areas that need a lot more (re) work. Amber indicates a 'middle of the road' average type assessment through to green which shows conformity and compliance to the standards set, and other positive traits such as a capability to do the job as well as the willingness to work with the processes and maybe even to go beyond that to help and act as an example to others.

Scoring quality in this way not only ensures there is no misunderstanding as to how assessment has taken place (as long as criteria accompanies it), but is also a way to show at a glance the level of compliance.

In previous organisations that I have worked, management have sometimes required (with project community knowledge) to see the results of audits in order to make decisions about areas around opportunities for promotion as well as furnishing the personal objectives review process, particularly when performance in projects has been linked to objectives.

Once a scoring assessment has been completed, it is wise to populate into a spread sheet or similar tracking tool that is then used for all future audits, to monitor what happens over time as a PMO metric to show:

- Indications of improvement
- Persistent lack of adherence or compliance
- Maturity growth (or lack of) in key areas and showing where focus needs to be applied

Having this information can not only provide assurance about projects in how they are doing today but can also furnish plans for improvement or recovery which is an added bonus of undertaking such an activity.

In Summary:

Scoring criteria is symbiotic with quality criteria; once you set what you require, you can then measure it. Measuring it enables decision making in areas that fall outside or within the parameters depending on the results.

Scoring in a visual way can provide benefits to both the PMO team and any key stakeholders that require access to the results by ensuring quick and easy interpretation.

Chapter 4

Creating the post-audit report

Once a project audit has been completed, it is sensible to record and track the results in order to measure compliance and capability over time but also to ensure that information is made readily available in an easy to see format to relevant stakeholders.

Caution should be exercised about who can see this report. If relevant key stakeholders request access, then auditees should be made aware that their results will not remain fully private. Where results are not requested from specific relevant key stakeholders, it is crucial to ensure the results are stored somewhere not accessible to the general public to maintain privacy. The PMO, if it is within their remit, should be dealing with any issues themselves by working closely with the project community and building positive relationships.

Recording results in a report (whether it is required by key relevant stakeholders or not) enables the PMO team to collectively understand the summary of the audit they have undertaken and what, if any, improvement measures are going to be implemented. Some or all team members may be involved in implementing those, so it is a good way to communicate that to the team. It can also help to compare the results of past audits and understand over time what is happening to maturity growth and the results of effective stakeholder engagement. Doing this can also help maturity and knowledge growth within the PMO.

The report should contain the following fields as a guide:

Introduction and Purpose
This section should introduce the audit, and explain why it is taking place. It should also describe the inputs and outputs; inputs being the data being examined coupled with the quality criteria necessary for assessment, and the outputs being the results of the audit. It should be short and to the point and may describe two primary purposes:

- The details in the report may be used to highlight the state of a project, a set of projects, the programme or the portfolio.

- The data may be used to highlight gaps, issues or provide recommendations for improvement or corrective action.

Objectives of the audit
This section should state the specific objectives of the audit. Common reasons for conducting an audit can include:

- Proof or disproving of suspected issues and the beginning of the journey to project recovery if they exist.

- Understanding what a project or set of projects is about, and what its health state is in order to establish an 'as-is' picture that considers any assumptions or constraints in order to form a 'to-be' roadmap for the PMO.

- Giving assurance to key relevant stakeholders about the state of a project, a programme or a portfolio of projects.

- As part of regular operational activity within the PMO.

- To support metrics or maturity related data over time.

- To scrutinise the level of compliance or capability considering the current and available level of standards or governance.

- Provision of supplemental information to understand any gaps, missing processes and standards, and to furnish a plan for improvement .

Scope of the audit (what was included in the review and what wasn't and why)
The scope section will describe what is going to be included in the audit and what isn't. For example, if it is an audit of just one project, it should be explicitly stated here. It may include details about project size (mentioned in chapter one); i.e. the audit scope may only include medium and large sized projects or programmes. If size has not yet been determined for whatever reason, cost can be used as a basic guide for inclusion or exclusion from an audit (e.g. all projects over £50k will be included) although this is only recommended when a risk assessment has not yet been completed.

This section may also specifically include exclusions to the audit. Projects may be given concession not to be included in the audit, for example, if a Project Manager has only just started in the organisation, recently started managing a brand new project or has just taken over a project from someone else, to make it fair.

Quality criteria used

This section describes the quality criteria (discussed in chapter two) that will be used. A link standards stored centrally is normally acceptable to include in a report like this.

Assumptions and constraints

Assumptions and constraints in an audit can include (as an example):

- The assumption that all data required will be readily available.
- The assumption that all Project and Programme Managers have brought all relevant information up to date.
- The assumption that, particularly if the person leading the audit is new to the organisation, everyone has the same capability and understanding of the criteria required to be met.

All Project and Programme managers should be forewarned of an audit unless the purpose of the audit is to 'spot check' compliance for PMO eyes only.

Results of the audit - Assessment and conclusion

The assessment and conclusion section should include a copy of the results of the actual audit. If, for example, it was recorded in a spread sheet, then this should be embedded in the document or a link to that document should be provided.

A summary of findings should be included, and it depends entirely on the purpose of the audit and objectives as to how much detail to give here. Suggested areas include:

- Overall observations relating to specific process and standards adherence or compliance
- Overall observations relating to the quality of documentation and evidence provided
- Overall observations about capability (it is particularly important to keep the report as confidential as possible if including this)
- What is happening or doesn't happen as a result of PMO standards or processes that are missing
- Areas that could be targeted for improvement
- Effectiveness of the current PMO and what to do about it
- Effectiveness of any supporting governance or interfaces such as Finance and Procurement
- Actions for the PMO or actions the PMO has taken to address any issues that have come out of the audit
- Actions for any other stakeholder (e.g. decisions required by senior stakeholders, line managers or team managers).

Addressing issues

Be mindful of the controversy that a report like this can cause, which is obviously dependent on the reasons for doing it in the first place, as well as the current organisational political challenges. People are likely to be sensitive if there is a hint of criticism and so it is very important to stick to the facts in any discussion and ensure that it does not get personal.

When addressing any issues with individuals, this should be approached sensitively one on one, and never in front of or with a group (including with more than one PMO member, even if the purpose for the accompanying PMO member to be there is for training).

As previously suggested, keeping results as confidential as possible is the best way forward and only ensure that the relevant and minimal amount of eyes get to see the results of any report.

For targeted project recovery, specific actions can be generated which PMO team members can address. It is worth bearing in mind that most if not all Project Managers will want to work with what the organisation requires, and if there is a lack of compliance, there may be a good reason for it. It is vital that the PMO has an understanding that there may be hidden information rather than jumping to any conclusions.

Once the 'as-is' picture is known, the 'to-be' roadmap can be put together, with targeted actions within a PMO plan if necessary or required.

In Summary:

- A report is always recommended to be created at the end of an audit.

- It should be shared with the minimum amount of people possible (if it should be shared at all) and only when necessary or specifically requested. Even then, if a report is requested, anyone subject to an audit should be informed to give them a chance to prepare and understand the result of any output.

- Issues should be addressed sensitively and always one on one. The PMO should attempt to resolve issues themselves and only escalate when issues persist.

- Results should be saved over time to understand growth (or lack of) in particular areas and to target particular areas where required.

Epilogue

. . . .

This book is designed as a resource for the PMO team in implementing an informal, internal project audit and reviewing quality in projects.

Hopefully this book has demonstrated how an audit can be a very useful and necessary tool in the PMO repository to provide assurance and management information needed for the performance of projects.

It is recommended that they are carried out at least every three months (I tend to do it once a month with mini audits at every gate review) with a complimentary set of other metrics to provide valuable information about project execution and delivery.

An audit spreadsheet template, which contains the guide quality criteria and questions that can be asked when undertaking an audit from this book, is available at my website for free here: http://www.pmosynergy.com/pmo-management---audit-x17592.html.

I hope you have found this book useful. I always welcome feedback on the contents and I can be contacted through www.pmosynergy.com.

Glossary

. . . .

Auditee

A person (or rather their provision and production of evidence (including documentation) of activity on a project) who is audited.

Auditor

A person or group who performs an audit.

Baseline

The line in the sand; the place from which everything else is measured thereafter in order to make a comparison.

Business as Usual (BAU)

Normal operational day to day organisational activity that is repeatable and on-going.

Control Techniques

Key and specific ways and techniques to manage a piece of change which involve tracking, managing, and monitoring elements of the project that may threaten the delivery of its objectives.

Enterprise PMO

A PMO that spans across the top of the organisation, incorporating IT and the Business into its remit to deliver business wide portfolio and resource management, governance, project standards and control.

Full governance vs. light touch governance	Once an assessment has been reached about a project's size and complexity, the PMO has to determine what types of governance, rigour and amount of PMO focus is appropriate relevant to that size. Applying a 'light governance' framework means auditing using superficial audit criteria and is usually reserved for smaller or less risky pieces of work. Applying a 'full governance' framework means using more deep-dive audit criteria, usually reserved for larger pieces of work where greater assurance is required.

Where you would use full governance and ask every single question, going through every single gate, auditing and asking for the production of all documentation required in the methodology and obtaining full approval at all required points, light touch mainly ends up being (but is not necessarily limited to) setting minimum gate review meetings that Project Managers should present at and attend, setting minimum documentation to be completed and reviewed at a high level during the lifecycle, and setting the governance approval and escalation procedures they are

	still required to go through (if any).
Governance	Provides clarity around roles, responsibilities, accountabilities, as well as organisational/departmental and decision making structures.
Health (as in project, programme or portfolio)	Health, usually assessed through the overall RAG is an indicator of how well a project is doing during its delivery taking into account many factors including project spend against the agreed budget and project delivery against the originally agreed schedule.
Maturity	Maturity in project management is the ability to repeat project delivery success and minimise failure through continual improvement, standardisation and optimisation to process, methodology and ways of working.
Pipeline	A picture of future demand, it is the projects and programmes that stakeholders require to be delivered in the future.
PMO	The word 'PMO' stands for 'Project, Programme, or Portfolio Management Office' and performs different functions depending on

the level it is set at and the requirements of management and the organisation.

According to the Axelos global best practice standard 'P3O', (based in the UK), PMO's 'provide a decision-enabling/delivery support model for all business change within an organisation...(and) create (s) tailored governance and support structures for managing portfolios, programmes and projects'.

PMO 'levels'

Describes different categories of PMO which can be focussed at either a project level, a programme level, a portfolio or enterprise level. Project and programme level offices are temporary (in line with the duration of the project or programme) and portfolio offices are permanent. PMO's at enterprise level are also permanent and normally recognised as portfolio centre of excellence offices, although other PMO's can contain centre of excellence attributes.

Project

A requirement to deliver an output that then brings benefits using a constrained amount of resource (cost and people) and time. Projects have a defined beginning and end point and is the reason why they are temporary.

Project Community	All people involved with projects, including Project, Programme and Portfolio Managers and their teams.
Programme	A programme is made up of a specific set of related projects (and therefore outputs) using constrained resource, that contributes to delivering an outcome aligned to an organisations' strategic objectives. Benefits will be brought at both the project and programme level. A programme can span many years depending on the change being delivered and is temporary.
Portfolio	A portfolio is made up of an assessed and prioritised selection of projects and programmes using constrained resource that all contribute to delivering an organisations' strategic objectives. Assessment is on-going, and projects can be stopped or paused if a change will no longer deliver the required benefits and value. A portfolio function is permanent - the projects and programmes within that portfolio are temporary.
P3M3	P3M3 is the portfolio, programme and project management maturity model. Downloadable for free at

https://www.axelos.com/best-practice-solutions/p3m3, it is a method of self assessment so that an organisation can understand its current level of maturity in project, programme or portfolio management, understand where the gaps are and work towards achieving higher levels of maturity by filling those gaps.

RAG

Stands for 'Red, Amber, Green' and is the coloured indicator backed up with specific criteria to assess the health of a particular area (e.g. the whole project, a risk, plan on track etc....)

Stakeholder

A stakeholder is a relevant person who may have an interest, influence on, concern about, participates in or is affected by something (e.g. changes, activities, process and actions).

Strategy and strategic objectives

Strategy is a future or long term plan to maximise organisational success. Strategic objectives are the goals that define what that success looks like.

Strategic alignment

If the benefits, outputs, and outcomes that a project or programme delivers contributes to strategic objectives, the project or programme is considered to be strategically aligned.

Acknowledgements

. . . .

I would like to say a huge thank you to everyone I have ever worked with over the years for helping my experience to grow and helping me to come to conclusions and find different solutions for ways to manage a PMO. I am ever grateful for being shown different paths, different ways, challenges and positive steps forward.

I also want to thank the amazing people that have worked directly for me over the years (you know who you are). I have been very lucky to work with such talented people.

In particular, I specifically want to thank Sadeeyah Akhtar and James Richards for providing professional opinions and expertise to some of the key elements of this book.

Index

Printed in Poland
by Amazon Fulfillment
Poland Sp. z o.o., Wrocław